MW01601043

Picture book of
NORWAY

Beautiful fjords, mountains, landscapes and towns
in the Scandinavian country Norway.

Lofoten

Trondheim

Hamnoy fishing village on Lofoten islands

Ålesund

Oslo

Oslo

Trolltunga

Bergen

The old bridge in Trondheim

Geiranger fjord

Andenes lighthouse

Lofoten

Northen lights over Lofoten

Stavanger

Stave church in Lillehammer

Stavanger

Brige over the river at Sjoa in Jotunheim

Kjeragbolten

Domkirke church in Fredrikstad

Lofoten

Oslo

Stavanger

Holmenkollen

Tromso

Oslo parliament building

Kjeragbolten

Northen lights over Lofoten

Bergen

Ålesund

Tromso hillside

Train in Flam

Oslo town hall

Lofoten

Geiranger

Church on Traena island

Hardanger

Oslo

National theater Oslo